AF437523

OCEAN
DAILY
PLANNER

THIS PLANNER BELONGS TO:

____

____

____

PLANNER FOR THE WEEK OF:

PLANNER FOR THE WEEK OF:

PLANNER FOR THE WEEK OF:

PLANNER FOR THE WEEK OF:

PLANNER FOR THE WEEK OF:

PLANNER FOR THE WEEK OF:

PLANNER FOR THE WEEK OF:

PLANNER FOR THE WEEK OF:

PLANNER FOR THE WEEK OF:
M
Monday
T
Tuesday
W
Wednesday
T
Thursday
F
Friday

PLANNER FOR THE WEEK OF:

PLANNER FOR THE WEEK OF:

PLANNER FOR THE WEEK OF:

PLANNER FOR THE WEEK OF:
M
Monday
T
Tuesday
W
Wednesday
T
Thursday
F
Friday

PLANNER FOR THE WEEK OF:

PLANNER FOR THE WEEK OF:

M
Monday

T
Tuesday

W
Wednesday

T
Thursday

F
Friday

PLANNER FOR THE WEEK OF:

PLANNER FOR THE WEEK OF:

PLANNER FOR THE WEEK OF:

M Monday

T Tuesday

W Wednesday

T Thursday

F Friday

PLANNER FOR THE WEEK OF:

PLANNER FOR THE WEEK OF:

PLANNER FOR THE WEEK OF:

M
Monday

T
Tuesday

W
Wednesday

T
Thursday

F
Friday

PLANNER FOR THE WEEK OF:

PLANNER FOR THE WEEK OF:

PLANNER FOR THE WEEK OF:

PLANNER FOR THE WEEK OF:

PLANNER FOR THE WEEK OF:

PLANNER FOR THE WEEK OF:

PLANNER FOR THE WEEK OF:
M
Monday
T
Tuesday
W
Wednesday
T
Thursday
F
Friday

PLANNER FOR THE WEEK OF:

PLANNER FOR THE WEEK OF:

PLANNER FOR THE WEEK OF:
M
Monday
T
Tuesday
W
Wednesday
T
Thursday
F
Friday

PLANNER FOR THE WEEK OF:

PLANNER FOR THE WEEK OF:

PLANNER FOR THE WEEK OF:

PLANNER FOR THE WEEK OF:

PLANNER FOR THE WEEK OF:

PLANNER FOR THE WEEK OF:

PLANNER FOR THE WEEK OF:

PLANNER FOR THE WEEK OF:

PLANNER FOR THE WEEK OF:

PLANNER FOR THE WEEK OF:

PLANNER FOR THE WEEK OF:
M
Monday
T
Tuesday
W
Wednesday
T
Thursday
F
Friday

PLANNER FOR THE WEEK OF:

M — Monday

T — Tuesday

W — Wednesday

T — Thursday

F — Friday

PLANNER FOR THE WEEK OF:

Monday

Tuesday

Wednesday

Thursday

Friday

PLANNER FOR THE WEEK OF:
M
Monday
T
Tuesday
W
Wednesday
T
Thursday
F
Friday

PLANNER FOR THE WEEK OF:

PLANNER FOR THE WEEK OF:
M
Monday
T
Tuesday
W
Wednesday
T
Thursday
F
Friday

PLANNER FOR THE WEEK OF:

PLANNER FOR THE WEEK OF:

PLANNER FOR THE WEEK OF:

PLANNER FOR THE WEEK OF:
M
Monday
T
Tuesday
W
Wednesday
T
Thursday
F
Friday

PLANNER FOR THE WEEK OF:

PLANNER FOR THE WEEK OF:

PLANNER FOR THE WEEK OF:

PLANNER FOR THE WEEK OF:

PLANNER FOR THE WEEK OF:

PLANNER FOR THE WEEK OF:

PLANNER FOR THE WEEK OF:

PLANNER FOR THE WEEK OF:

PLANNER FOR THE WEEK OF:
M
Monday
T
Tuesday
W
Wednesday
T
Thursday
F
Friday

PLANNER FOR THE WEEK OF:

PLANNER FOR THE WEEK OF:
M
Monday
T
Tuesday
W
Wednesday
T
Thursday
F
Friday

PLANNER FOR THE WEEK OF:

PLANNER FOR THE WEEK OF:

PLANNER FOR THE WEEK OF:

PLANNER FOR THE WEEK OF:
M
Monday
T
Tuesday
W
Wednesday
T
Thursday
F
Friday

PLANNER FOR THE WEEK OF:

PLANNER FOR THE WEEK OF:

PLANNER FOR THE WEEK OF:

PLANNER FOR THE WEEK OF:

PLANNER FOR THE WEEK OF:

PLANNER FOR THE WEEK OF:
M
Monday
T
Tuesday
W
Wednesday
T
Thursday
F
Friday

PLANNER FOR THE WEEK OF:

PLANNER FOR THE WEEK OF:

PLANNER FOR THE WEEK OF:
M
Monday
T
Tuesday
W
Wednesday
T
Thursday
F
Friday

PLANNER FOR THE WEEK OF:
M
Monday
T
Tuesday
W
Wednesday
T
Thursday
F
Friday

PLANNER FOR THE WEEK OF:

PLANNER FOR THE WEEK OF:

PLANNER FOR THE WEEK OF:

PLANNER FOR THE WEEK OF:
M
Monday
T
Tuesday
W
Wednesday
T
Thursday
F
Friday

PLANNER FOR THE WEEK OF:

M Monday

T Tuesday

W Wednesday

T Thursday

F Friday

PLANNER FOR THE WEEK OF:

PLANNER FOR THE WEEK OF:

PLANNER FOR THE WEEK OF:

PLANNER FOR THE WEEK OF:

PLANNER FOR THE WEEK OF:

PLANNER FOR THE WEEK OF:

PLANNER FOR THE WEEK OF:

PLANNER FOR THE WEEK OF:

PLANNER FOR THE WEEK OF:

PLANNER FOR THE WEEK OF:

PLANNER FOR THE WEEK OF:
M
Monday
T
Tuesday
W
Wednesday
T
Thursday
F
Friday

PLANNER FOR THE WEEK OF:

PLANNER FOR THE WEEK OF:
M
Monday
T
Tuesday
W
Wednesday
T
Thursday
F
Friday

PLANNER FOR THE WEEK OF:

M Monday

T Tuesday

W Wednesday

T Thursday

F Friday

PLANNER FOR THE WEEK OF:

PLANNER FOR THE WEEK OF:
M
Monday
T
Tuesday
W
Wednesday
T
Thursday
F
Friday

PLANNER FOR THE WEEK OF:
M
Monday
T
Tuesday
W
Wednesday
T
Thursday
F
Friday

PLANNER FOR THE WEEK OF:

OCEAN
DAILY
PLANNER